LOVE AFTER SAPPHO

LOVE AFTER SAPPHO

Peter Abbs

halfcrown

halfacro♛n

First published in Great Britain in 1999
by halfacrown publishers
198 Victoria Avenue
Kingston upon Hull HU5 3DY

Printed in Great Britain by
Copytech UK, Peterborough

© Peter Abbs

No part of this publication may be reproduced, stored in a retrieval system, or transmitted, in any form or by any means, electronic, mechanical, photocopying, recording or otherwise, without the prior permission of the publisher.

This book is sold subject to the condition that it shall not, by way of trade or otherwise, be lent, resold, hired out or otherwise circulated without the publisher's prior consent in any form of binding or cover other than that in which it is published and without a similar condition including this condition being imposed on the subsequent purchaser.

ISBN 0 9537022 19

This copy is one of the first 100 copies of the print run.

Acknowledgements

Acknowledgements are due to the editors of the following magazines in which some of these poems first appeared:

Acumen,
Agenda,
Dark Horse,
Interpreter's House,
Jewish Quarterly,
Poetry Wales,
The Review, and
South.

for

D

CONTENTS

PROLOGUE	1
Navigating Darkness	2
POST-MODERN LOVE	3
First Fall-Out	4
Kamikase Stars	5
A Bleeding Wreath	6
Las Vegas Perhaps	7
Love in a Shopping Mall	8
Love Anywhere	9
Speaking of Eros	10
A Mantra of Accidental Light	11
A Violent Cleansing	12
At Cuckmere Estuary	13
LAST RITES	15
At Cromer Hospital	16
All Night in Hospital	17
Travelling to a Foreign Land	18
Extreme Unction	19
At the Old House	20
On Sheringham Beach	21
A Girl in Sepia	22
LOVE'S LABOUR	23
Possession	24
Incomparable Beauty	25
In Sappho's Museum	26
Let us Live and Love	27
Not Catullus	28
The Marriage of True Minds	29
Love's Unicorn	30
Girl with a Flute	31
Philip Larkin without Love	32
A Metaphysical Sappho	33
Alchemists down the Age	34

DESCENDANTS OF THE FIREBALL — 35
Under the Burning Sycamore — 36
Pisces — 37
Dark with Snow — 38
Jewels of Consciousness — 39
Descendants of the Fireball — 40
A Brief Excess — 41
Love after Sappho — 42
Towards the Divine — 43

LA VITA NUOVA — 45
The Naming of Things — 46
On a Journey — 47
The Aura of our Face — 48
Massage — 49
Saturday Day-School — 50
The Waterfall — 51
Sprigs of Rosemary — 52
Le Ballon Rouge — 53
And what is Transcendence? — 54

THE DANCE OF SYLLABLES — 55
A White Dark-Scented Rose — 56
Moments of Being — 57
A Symphony of Sound — 58
Ave Gratia Plena — 59
The Dance of Syllables — 60
Inner Fugue — 61
Then Love me for my Flying — 62
The Song of Words — 63

CODA — 65
Six Epiphanies — 66

PROLOGUE

She could not remember anything but longing
Sappho

Navigating Darkness

Sometimes I think of us: obscure spiders
Spinning from our entrails metaphysical webs,
Acrobats who hang from a single thread

Dancing awkwardly to silk the sullen emptiness,
To weave together disparate things, leaf and ledge,
Branch and bridge, the vital and the dead.

Our fragile geometries shimmer over the abyss.
Or sometimes I see us through another image:
That athletic girl on a warm Minoan hill;

Upside down, she somersaults the charging bull -
A red speck of transcendence against the blue.
A mere child. Inviolable. Free. And falling still.

And then I think of Sappho: *the lightest breath*
Yet my words live on – in the acoustic chambers
Of our mind's navigating darkness beyond the stars.

POST-MODERN LOVE

I do not know what way to move; I am of two minds
                                                    Sappho

First Fall-Out

We woke early and on the window saw this labyrinth:
Seeded ferns. Feathered grass. Bridges.
Domes. Spires. Pyramids.

Love, you said, *this is our looking-glass.*
This is our ancient city and our inner maze.
The story of our lives is written here.

But as we gazed the sun came up
A blistering and a burning orange.
It melts our world, dissolves our city –

And all the names we whispered; *fern, grass,*
Bridge, dome, spire, pyramid slide down the glass
Like tears – like pain – like Hiroshima – like Nagasaki.

Our kissing now is cruel and bitter.
First Fall-Out. First Nuclear Winter.

Kamikase Stars

Brutal in the heart of August winter slips in,
Strips the green foliage, burns the green leaves.
Cool on my brow. Cold on your fingers.

An oil drum flares without a sound.
Pyramids of skulls rise from the smoking ground.
A war-lord patrols his cardboard town.

Insubstantial ghost I pace the wooden floor.
What for? What ultimately for?
Our lacerating days go out like all the others.

The guru in the Book of Wisdom speaks:
Throw the dice twice – then leave it to the play of chance.
The kamikase stars blaze into the infinite.

Divided lovers, where are we?
Under the smouldering rubble. Under the burning sea.

A Bleeding Wreath

Now we stare both ways across the divide,
Lonely together, paradoxical, Janus-eyed.
There's no holding back the jagged tide –

Its salt-serrated edges, its undertow, its minute
By minute, fierce ebbing back and out.
We shiver as we kiss, drown as we doubt.

Our age is a tip of abandoned faiths. Nothing's secure.
The currents are murderous on this modern shore –
They have taken other drifting lives before

With no disgorging of the bodies from their depths;
And there are no gods left to lay a bleeding wreath
For the sundering of marriage – suddenness of death.

Las Vegas Perhaps

There's this city I am driving to. Las Vegas –
Perhaps. Its gaudy beads of light seduce,
Release adrenalin. I'm in a stolen car
And travelling fast. Suddenly, it blows a tyre.
The vehicle somersaults, bursts into fire.
I scramble out – my hair's ablaze – and shout –
For Christ's sake help. The traffic neither stops
Nor brakes. The drivers turn their ghostly heads –
And then accelerate... Love, there are no words
For dreams like this. They detonate the mind.
Where was I running from?
What was I running for?
This numbing loss – this age-old fear.
Tell me I still exist... Stroke my burning hair.

Love in a Shopping Mall

Here's a place Dante would fail to recognize –
Though a leopard leaps the merchandise.

So let me stroke your hair and kiss your lips –
Justice and Love decay under our finger-tips.

The clock's electronic hands rotate in silence.
Tampax – Freedom. Vodka – Love. Ideal – ZX.

The latest Volvo cruises to the music of Elgar.
Paradise for Men. Always Coca-Cola –

A body smoulders in the dust.
The black child from El Fau stares out at us.

How to speak when the words lack weight –
And all the images are counterfeit?

Under the glare of lights – in the eyeless maze,
In the huge wreckage of our days.

Love Anywhere

Restless under the world's flight paths –
Hong Kong – Jakarta – Singapore – Tel Aviv.
All night silver planes thunder across tarmac
Then float between the amber and the black.
In offices above our jaded heads capital
Crosses time zones, Multi-Nationals totter,
Revive and crash. The global clichés jag
Across five-laned motorways. The faxes judder in.
At six a.m. the breakfast chat begins.
We turn to each other with shameless needs –
We fuck to ease our jet-lagged skin –
Then fall away to ancient dreams:
Caliban smirks. Ariel chants on her heap of bones –
As jets take off, as deficits cross time zones.

Speaking of Eros

Gilded, you said, they were gilded by love;
It was as if when they smiled the gods above
Poured honey over them. Their limbs were gold
And shone transparent. As you spoke a cold

Sweat broke over me. I knew if I had the power
I would have had them executed in the public square,
Hung, drawn, quartered or crucified upside down,
Their honeyed limbs dragged over common ground –

And would have shredded all lies in their defence,
For ease of civilization requires a formal reticence.
Then later came those swarming flies –
Buzzing through my mouth, my ears, my socket-eyes.

A Mantra of Accidental Light

Time has no purpose, but you come again
To grace my life. Love's jaded jargon cries
On my tongue, bitter with past betrayals,
Ancient battles, festered scars, tabloid lies.

Love's a plastic tag on merchandise
And Eros a pornographer. Under every word
An angel bleeds, dragged from the arching sky,
And raped and blinded. Cupid, you have become

A crazed, degraded thing – a crass hard-on
For every predilection. Who now can speak of
Love's celestial influence? Today I return
Your steadfast glance without a word.

The furnace sun is bronze upon your hair.
A mantra of accidental light. A form of prayer.

A Violent Cleansing

We woke last night to hear the bitter rain
Scouring the slates, flaying the window pane,
Flooding the dark river. After a long dry spell
Such a savage cleansing. And as we fell
Into uneasy sleep I sensed the driven rain
Wash our sprawling polluted cities clean.
A single ablution through the slow black hours.
A brute force the wind rampaged the streets
Clawing the seductive eyes, the simulated smiles,
The glittering masks of affluence – while
A pitiless icy rain erased the lexicon
Of power, insidious betrayals, soft jargon.
Love, when the new dawn's morning breaks
With pristine beauty, do not rush to speak.

At Cuckmere Estuary

We stand on the shingle as night comes in. Behind us
Storm clouds, bruised and red, slump to the Downs. This is
The last violence of the haemorrhaging sun. Lightning forks

And flickers vertical at the edge. All that our eclectic times
Have claimed dissolves. We listen to a silence whose signs
Are hard and hazardous to read. We are novices. New-comers.

Inland a siren wails and spreads its shrill alarm. At last
The stillness returns more intensely reticent for the dissonance.
The reason is... The reason is... There are no reasons left:

Platitudes jostle in the gaps. The healing word takes flight
In the daily battle-ground of microphones and hype
And singing Orpheus drowns in a flood of camera light.

We close our eyes and sense the breeze against our flesh.
The salt burns our mouths. There's no desire to talk. We drink
In the forgotten dark. The tide spumes white against the chalk.

LAST RITES

But all must be endured

                                                Sappho

At Cromer Hospital

Mother, I sit powerless by your bed.
Crouched under newly laundered sheets,
Your body has shrunk to that of a child.
Your face is cracked, eyes blue as cornflowers.
You shouldn't have come all that way to see me;
I'm alright... A few days left to live, self-effacing
As ever. Though you can barely lift a child's
Beaker to your lips, you ask for barley water.
The drip-feed's off; there'll be no more solids.
Once, I'd have done anything for you;
A timid boy, I loved you to excess.
Outside the ward June's burning laburnum
Spills on the world a fading radiance.
The morphine zips in to ease the dying.

All Night in Hospital

All night in hospital I hold your hand
And ache to sleep. Unread newspapers litter
Your room. Unwanted food, unwanted drink
Stand on the window sill. Here time neither ticks
Nor moves but hangs silent and oppressive.
A patient in another ward screams out – a flurry
Of movement – a metal trolley clatters down
An unseen corridor. In an urgent track of time
Someone, somewhere, is dying. Almost dawn –
Outside the senile day begins. Birds repeat
Their morning platitudes, blank clouds gather.
Grotesquely the sun breaks through. Mother,
What can we place against such huge indifference?
A hand across the skull. Love's glance. This breath.

Travelling to a Foreign Land

And now flowers in their glass cases burn
With furious incandescence. Red. Yellow.
Blue. Absurdly beautiful.
I hold your frail veined hands,
Put vaseline on your lips, lavender water
On your brow. Our final ritual. You slip
Into sleep, stir, start to hallucinate.
Strange animals stalk the place. Silver spoons
Rise in the room and then, an oracle, you speak;
Feelings are hard to portray... You must understand
The other view... It's like travelling to a foreign land.
Mother, I have never heard you quite so eloquent.
I squeeze your hands and kiss your dried out lips –
As the vessel of our lives drifts to the precipice.

Extreme Unction

Today the priest arrives. He holds the crucifix
For you to kiss. He makes the sign of Christ
Upon your frowning brow, your dried-out lips.
I stand awkward. I cannot kneel nor say
Amen... As a child I prayed for life eternal;
Now life dissolves under our finger-tips.
We lurch to our extinction. And die alone.
This is the poison which blisters the skin;
This is the chemical which corrodes the bone.
Holy Mary, Mother of God, pray for us
Sinners now and at the hour of our death –
At the end of taste – at the end of touch –
At the end of speech – at the end of breath –

At the Old House

Last night I slept at the old house alone.
Half ghost, half insomniac, I thought
Of all the wasted hours we spent there,
Uncut, unharvested, unbound.
What was I hoping for? A moment to gather in
The stunted crop? Memory gave little back.
Outside a blank moon hurtled through the black.
Today I visit your unsettled grave.
The wreaths have gone, their flimsy ribbons
Lie on the earth, silk-blue and shimmering.
What else remains? A scorched rectangle of turf
Where a cavity had been. A nameless ache
Beneath the aching skin. No clear horizon.
An implacable sky. A growing emptiness within.

On Sheringham Beach

I walk today's decaying line of flesh and bone:
How to redeem the mean apotheosis of time,
The endless drift, the detritus and waste?
Here at seventeen I strolled reciting Hopkins
To the waves, Wordsworth's poems in my pocket –
A talisman against the age. I was drunk on words,
Dizzy on their acoustic arcs of sound.
What time brings time terminates.
On the promenade old men eye the altercations
Of the tide. It daily rises to withdraw
And spews its dead upon the shore.
Above the casual slaughter the sky recedes
Into a blank infinitude where gulls,
Like apparitions, scream – then drop into oblivion.

A Girl in Sepia

Mother, there's still a bitterness on my tongue
And iron rusts near my heart. It's hell
To speak the truth. With you, I seldom did.
Absurdly shy, I was the kind of child who stared
And stuttered, to find long after the event the words
He hungered for. Tonight I look through photographs;
Here you are, a girl – in sepia – your First Communion:
All curls and frills. And here you are – in black and white –
Eighteen. Young. And vulnerable. And beautiful.
And here decades later – in Kodak colour –
The small, huddled, stubborn woman I remember.
I still wince before your flawed, excessive love;
Yet now, far too late, beyond the grave –
Ache to thank you – for the life you gave.

LOVE'S LABOUR

I think that someone will remember us in another time.
                                                    Sappho

Possession

After Sappho

– just like a god – that man –
who sits over there –
all eyes – all ears –
falling for your every word –

when I glance at both of you –
fire gashes my neck –
sweat oozes from my hair –
the words jam –

my tongue is splintered glass –
I see only blackness –
in my drumming ears
Syracuse crashes –

I am white ash
at the boundaries of death –
motes of dust
in the lashing gale –

I am as free
as the moth driven
into the scorching wick –
into the burning flame –

Incomparable Beauty

Once more, incomparable beauty burns my skin.
I am a delta of fire.
Aphrodite loosen my limbs!

Who said there could be no more love poetry?
For each day some-one, somewhere,
Falls into love's vortex. Is half dismembered,

Half encompassed there. Chill douses his spine,
Sweat glues his hair. And all around
Swirls apprehension. A man, near drowning, dreads

The depth of water he no longer treads. To compare
It to the nakedness of birth, the completeness
Of death, the radiance of gods is hardly to start.

It is the long insomniac nights. Tears
Jagging the eyes. The stammering heart.

In Sappho's Museum

Here love's scribble is kept at calibrated temperatures –
Written circa: carbon dating suggests: the expert infers.

The scholar's fingers slide nervously across the lids
Making notes, transpositions, a hundred *op cits* and *ibids*.

Love fades into a list of facts and figures. The crazed senses
Are dust under a pile of papers, translations, conferences.

Who now can feel the salt tears staining the papyri, the din
Of jealousy rocking the skull, love tattooing the taut skin?

Let us Live and Love

After Catullus

Come, Lesbia, let us live and love –
Nor give a damn what old farts say.
The sinking sun will rise again –
But when our blaze is out –

It's over. So give me a thousand kisses.
Another hundred! A thousand more!
Till breathless we can count no more –
Then let us mock tomorrow's pen-pushers,

Academics, smart-arse critics
Who'll freeze our lust in lists and figures.
How the ticker tape reels from their lips!
Jargon. Acronyms. Facts. Classificatory lists:

Catullus, Gaius, Valerius. Etcetera. Circa. Idem.
Master of iambics. Fuck the lot of them!

Not Catullus

How is it with me? Not good. You must
Understand one thing. I am a liberal without
A creed. The clock ticks slowly in my room.
At night I watch the bald moon ride the sky.
The starving cat yowls at my bedroom door;
The damp tattoos my Laura Ashley walls.
Each morning I switch on the radio and take
My pills. At seven a.m. the bills slide in.
I often forget to replace the light bulbs
When they go. The house grows darker.
Yesterday I did not draw the curtains back
But standing by the mantelpiece scrawled
In the dust: *I need to love, I need to be loved.*
I rubbed it out at once. Of course.

The Marriage of True Minds

Jan van Eyck painted the Arnolfini Marriage in 1434.
For Annabel and Matthew

Here married love is memorable. It has the clarity
Of light filling a Dutch interior to announce
The virtues of the real, grace in what is ordinary.
This candelabra. This bed. Four ripe oranges.
Consider the movement of the bridegroom's hands:
How the right one is raised as if to bless
While the left reaches out to reassure.
A marriage of seriousness and tenderness.
And the encompassing pattern of their love
Is everywhere; the dark green of the wedding dress
Against the red, one flickering candle above
Their temperate heads, the shaggy terrier at their toes.
And the convex mirror on the distant wall,
A lover's gazing eye, reflects it all.

Love's Unicorn

Somewhat after Rilke

It never was. It never ran through tall grass.
It never tasted ice water on its tongue.
It never felt the salt wind nipping the nape of its neck.
It never saw the whiteness of its body.
It never was. It could never be.

Then, one day, you longed for its existence.
Slowly it emerged, intangibly it came.
It moved in the shadows, hovered in the soul's undergrowth
Its nostrils quivered, its clean eyes opened –
As if waiting for you to call its name.

And suddenly you said the secret word: *unicorn*!
A single horn broke from its stark brow.
Startlingly white. Precise. Spiralling to a point.
Ah! It existed then – in the silver mirror of your longing.
And that which never was, became.

Girl with a Flute

I think today of Osip Mandelstam at the edge
Of his charred life, pacing the streets of Voronezh,
A scorched bird locked in an iron cage,
Small head, tilted back, screaming his rage:
I am the tree-splitting storm – rain zig-zagging the glass –
The gargoyle frothing with water – Dante, Villon, Mozart –
The open mouth of God. Drawn to they know-not-what
The town kids jeer and shout: *General! General!* – but
Soon they will be mouthing his satirical songs,
His anti-Soviet doubt, his musical codas –
Each poem a mantra of defiant breath
Against the status quo, against his martyr's death.
What to think now? What cause should one salute?
A cadence in the wind. A girl with a flute.

Peter Abbs

Philip Larkin without Love

I live at the end of a long line into loneliness –
Distrusting high phrases, the clichés of redress.
I inspect flat land, allotments, survey the dead.
I envy everybody everything. If I cast my bread

On the waters it would sink as heavily as stone.
How the grave hurtles towards us. I exist alone.
How far back do we have to go? How many stations
Of denial? How many fathers, mothers, relations

Blowing ash into our stuttering mouth – ash on
Our tongue – ash on the water – ash on the sun.
And where do our private holocausts begin –
In the privations of love or the aimless gene?

And, once broken, what can make us whole?
Oh, terra incognita! Oh, dark night of the soul!

A Metaphysical Sappho;
On Reading Gillian Rose's *Love's Work*

For David Evans

And every sentence thrown out's a baited hook
To catch the drifting intellect – to hurl it back
Into its turbulent element, but deeper down and

Further out. There's no softness in this glinting book.
We're born askew. Wounded. Inherently off-track.
All life's a mess and love's dialectical. We're bound

To fail, so let's fail well – take on the eloquence
Of plunging dolphins or hunted whales that sing
In bloody water their strange and piercing psalms:

I will stay in the revel of ideas and risk;
Learning, failing, wooing, grieving, trusting, working, reposing –
In this sin of language and lips...

Keep your mind in hell and despair not. Stand free
In the broken middle. You did. And failed us – brilliantly.

Alchemists down the Age

This is the beginning of a poem. It is a vessel
For disparate things. Each day brings an element,
Unclassified, raw, incalcitrant. Car crash,

A burning head, glass. The lilac massing purple
At the window, a word in the discarded paper,
Stray threads of a marriage. Blood. Coriander. Ash.

Then the power's switched on. Flames lick the flask,
Blacken the base. Nothing's clear but the task;
The stirring, testing, tasting – that slow thickening

As the heat rips. What is it that I'm after?
An enduring amalgam that fuses the parts.
Was this the labour for gold? The philosopher's ring?

I think of alchemists down the age, god's poets –
Artisans working through the insomniac hours –
With burnt fingers, charred skin, cracked hands.

DESCENDANTS OF THE FIREBALL

Eros...sweet-bitter, impossible creature

                                              Sappho

Under the Burning Sycamore

We walk through the autumn wood. Time is the cadence
Of our falling steps, the rhythm of our passing.
What can assuage our transience –

So briefly breath condenses in the air. Shrivelled leaves
And twigs lodge in our clothes and streaming hair.
The Buddha says *All things pass*

Work on your life with diligence. When did he says these words?
Under what forsaken tree? And when did we stroll into
The smouldering wreckage of this wood?

Memories break, fade, go slack. Chrysanthemums shed
Their dark aroma; their crowns are packed with death.
A silence beats against my head

Its chill amnesia. We are spindrift prone to dream,
Our hours cremating into ash. Under the burning sycamore
The blackbird sings our requiem.

Pisces

We draw our astrological sign on sand
As the brackish tide comes in, crass lovers,
Imagining the world as ours – as if our hand
Could map love onto the burning planets,

Black holes, imploding stars. *In the beginning*
A vast explosion. An incomparable violence.
Then who are we? And where do we fit in?
Creatures of chaos, quirks of chance.

Our astrological signs are sealed and coded songs;
They cannot disclose the purpose of the galaxies
Nor grace this barren shore. Ceaseless tongues
Of salt erase our zodiacal scrawl.

Only inside our fraying lives these marks are more.
An unbounded surplus – not maps but metaphor.

Dark with Snow

All day white flakes circle the occluded sun,
Bits of nothing the ice wind has blindly shaped.
They mount on slate and twig and window sill.
The suburb's rubbed out, the world's a shroud –

Its violence stilled. We switch on the news:
Hazardous conditions. Northern cities at a standstill.
All main-line stations closed. Most motorways.
The freezing mist obliterates the amber light;

Our window's dark with driven white.
At four o'clock it's starless night.
Under the glass the bitterness seeps in.
Love, where are we in this rage of ice,

This eschatology of fading light, this ashen glow?
Our words make frantic marks across the snow.

Jewels of Consciousness

Love, listen – we exist to surpass ourselves,
To break the boundaries of our cells, *to cancel* –
To transcend! Nothing in nature tells us
Who we are. Consider the music of the spheres –
Random blips, distant howls, inhuman blurs.
Planets collide... Huge stars explode...
Black holes devour matter... Quasars implode.
Nature's a terrorist who enters fast. She decrees
The law of entropy to every part,
Scrubs clean the archives of the brain, with no heart,
For no purpose, for no God, for no justifying art –
Blots out memory, annuls the past.
So who are we in all of this? Small, dazzling
Jewels of consciousness – against the dark.

Descendants of the Fireball

Let me gaze upon the candour of your face,
Beautiful after so much grief and trace
Again your body's braille. Under intent
And moving finger-tips our lives seem eloquent –

Yet we stare down a contracting cone of time:
Man. Mammal. Mollusc. Amoeba. Slime.
Vast explosion. Unbridled violence.
And who are we in this ungentle universe?

Nothing returns our scanning gaze. Do we exist
To amaze ourselves, to leap the distance
Of the galaxies? *To cancel – to transcend*!
Even as we speak an exploding star sends

Light into an infinity no-one can read, nor comprehend.
Let us burn brightly against our end.

A Brief Excess

Listen, for one moment – life's precarious.
A choking gasp before uncertainties, a hyphen
Darting between two question marks,
Nor do the scattered stars at night enlighten

The grave's indelible reticence. Between
Mountains of ice we shape our metaphors
And from accident and chance make up a life –
Something cherished simply because it's chosen.

We are catherine wheels that whirr and spark,
A brief excess before the dark. Tomorrow
Slips beyond our grasp and history's over.
Each second steals the imprint of our lives.

The equivocal sun burns fiercely on our lips –
Against its cooling, let us kiss.

Love after Sappho

Who are we in this pitiless universe?
On the margins. At the edge. Precarious,
We stammer questions. Nothing answers.
Born in a ditch craving transcendence –
We're out of bounds. We're dispossessed.

Love has its place in the sun's brilliance –
Thus Sappho, as she scrawled and laughed
And kissed. Precise. Carnal. Consummate.
Not here – where the sun burns cancerous
And nameless galaxies rip into the infinite.

There's no exit, and there's no free flight.
The cormorant dives into a radioactive sea –
We make love under a sulphurous light –
And the Furies ascend more remorseless than Christ.

Towards the Divine

Obedience to the force of gravity. The greatest sin.
                                                    Simon Weil

We're at the edge of meaning here. *Almost –*
Almost... From the molecule and mollusc
To the music of Mozart, there's a gap.

This is the chasm where spirit is born
Or bleeds aborted. Where each twists to climb
The vertical drop, downward wall,

Drag of gravity. Here nature's deaf
To our screams and calls. Ours is the flight,
The jagged movement, defiance of law.

Into the blistering light we deliver
Our sighs, fears, psalms, prayers.
This is nature's terminus, life's unbroken abyss –

For the God we believe in has still to exist.

LA VITA NUOVA

Oltre la spera che più larga gira
passa 'l sospiro ch'esce del mio core:
intelligenza nova, che l'Amore
piangendo mette in lui, pur su lo tira.

Beyond the sphere turning with widest gyre
Out of my heart a sign ascends:
A new intelligence that weeping Love
Bestows attracts him ever higher.

Dante

The Naming of Things

Intimate stranger I name for you what things I can –
Demotic daisy, prophetic dandelion,

Jasmine, freesias, acanthus, saxifrage,
A litany of scattered names

Plucked from the hurricane of riven time,
Syllables to set against oblivion –

Their cadence rides our urgent breath
Flowering before the void of death –

Yet who can restore, what can atone
The melanoma of skin, the necrosis of bone,

Mind's alzheimers, cancer of doubt,
Sudden unmeaning, slackening, the blackening out?

Bewildered naming in the thick of time:
Demotic daisy. Prophetic dandelion.

On a Journey

On a journey I read of a future in which rancour
Played no part, where no trauma
Lifted the compulsive finger to pluck again the canker

Of the past and as I looked out of the window
I watched the Downs with their flow
Of dips and curves and it was as though what I saw

Was no more than the crystallizing dream of what I'd read:
Life choreographed to time. A horse cantered
In the wind. A gate opened into clouds. A crow blacked

Over my head. A white path zig-zagged into the unknown.
And listen, each thing said. *Nothing
Is ever the same again. Observe. Integrate. Transcend.*

The Aura of your Face

Who can describe the aura of your face?
A proof of the existence of God? Perhaps.
Today the sun's vertical light descends as grace

Through towering clouds to enlighten our late
Estrangement and I recall those Chinese paintings,
Long landscape scrolls, where in the firmament

Through rising scrawls of mist a small tree
Hangs over the abyss to blossom there – suddenly
White, frail, incomparable. Imago dei.

Massage

When your hands with a delicacy all their own
Hovered over my skin, caressing the dark hair,
Yielding to the hardness of cartilage and bone

I remembered my father in his brief old age,
Sour with self-loathing, hawking into the stove
The soft black mucus. In the incomprehensible cage

Of his marriage, a wounded animal, love's pariah,
Padding the hard floor, sniffing the medical air,
Alone and fearing the beginning of nowhere.

And I wept for the touch he had never known,
The hand easing the skin, soothing the terminal bone:
The panther, uncaged, in its darkness coming home.

Saturday Day-School

Last night racing for the train you left your watch;
This morning I pick it up and strap it to my wrist;
The dark leather releases the perfume of your flesh:
Frail, understated, intoxicating. All day as I teach

Your body lies next to mine, long Byzantine face, black eyes,
Your soft nipples slowly hardening into pink rose-hips.
I talk of the upsurge of time, sudden growth and risk.
I unstrap the scented watch and lay it on the desk.

The Waterfall

What happened between us? Almost nothing was said –
But our high trance snapped, the air became glacially cold.
In a fraction of a second the descending water froze
And its colour was grey like an eye about to close,

Clouding over, going entirely out of focus, monotone.
For the next two days I moved almost an automaton.
I couldn't believe it. The hurt hung hard in my eyes –
Behind mechanical lids there were long nails of ice.

But the second you sobbed on my equivocal shoulder
How quickly the thaw set in. The ice-spell was over.
Then came that indivisible waterfall curving over us,
Its raw music crashing into our ears, our moist eyes

Gleaming again. Always the same – forever changing.
Now its rainbow spray lights on our shivering skin.

Sprigs of Rosemary

I bring this sprig of rosemary; but what is rosemary for?
It is for releasing memory, for increasing memory's store.

Yet few memories come back; childhood oppresses
With its weight of sullen fears. My life regresses

Into the black. I cannot remember what I said or did.
A haphazard crow flies at an angle to the wood.

So many memories gone into the gap under the falling wave,
Ash to the metallic fire, the blankness of the grave.

There's a paradox here. I pluck rosemary to mark what's absent,
To acknowledge what is over with aromatic scent,

To let it go with grace – and then I remember images of you:
The lapis lazuli against the whiteness of your neck, your sigh

At the eternal candour of its blue. You are the one somewhere
In my imagination with sprigs of rosemary in her hair

And sprays of bay leaves in her hands, whose radiant eyes
Bring back, at memory's furthest root, the glint of Paradise.

Le Ballon Rouge

Do you remember how that Spring we talked of the Red Balloon?
How the boy we'd seen in the 60's film sauntered the streets
Of Paris, a divine child, a red balloon drifting above his head –

Rhapsodic as dreams, as light as breath. *Puer Aeternus*, we said –
You rushed to buy the translation of *Le Ballon Rouge*. The words
Danced in our dizzy heads. We gazed at the photographs. Soon

It became our tarot pack of images, our sudden New Testament
And we its willing votaries. Together we proclaimed the revolt
Of all captive balloons. Each day we woke under the sign of art

And levity; the Red Balloon joined Papegano, Krishna, Mozart.
And exactly where we said it would the kingfisher took flight –
As so often desire and chance flared into a single counterpoint:

All summer an epiphany of red and blue. We drove to Beachy Head
To watch the morning dawn, to see the sun rise from the dark.
You took a small red balloon and let it float over the cliff's stark

Edge. It was too dangerous to observe the slow arc of its descent –
And, then, do you remember how the sun came up a burning disc,
A perfect circle, staring red, the astonished eye of a returning god,

A divine child demanding recognition – a nativity of light and blood,
As if nothing was ever entirely lost and life rose from the dead –
And – do you remember now? – *I could worship it*, you said.

And what is Transcendence?

And what is transcendence? you said as the gale's wind
Hurled us up the bone-white brow of Beachy Head,
Powerless before its raging and then in the turbulence

High above you saw a single bird riding the chaos,
Gliding and rising and falling, a dancer in wilderness –
Storm its element. *Ah there*, we shouted, *transcendence!*

THE DANCE OF SYLLABLES

Come now my holy lyre
Find your voice and speak to me

                                                    Sappho

A White Dark-Scented Rose

Love, listen to these words that run obliquely,
That never quite declare their aims, nor yield
What they appear to promise. Strange. Haunted.

Labile. Remember, last night, how the dark wind
Blew the transfiguring snow across the Downs
Over the familiar dusty paths? Like that, but not

Like that at all. Or imagine a white dark-scented rose
In some unknown garden, petal by petal, silently
Opening, silently closing, and no God watching.

Like that, but not like that at all. These words
Rise on their cadence. They cast a further spell –
Until we enter an estrangement which feels like home.

Moments of Being

There are no axioms to silence critics –
There are only moments and metaphors
Which make the blood course faster for their stimulus.

They explode into imagination with such force
They create a firmament, a site for angels.
In our galactic skulls live all the gods.

And there's always the gift of language. Sudden speech.
Words which break the sullen water to cut
A silver track of dripping light

Or lift like calligraphic swifts into a holocaust sky
To scrawl their zig-zag stanzas –
As the moon rises and drifts. Silent.

Eucharistic.
White.

A Symphony of Sound

What is true is incommensurable.
It is the epileptic child born in a stable.
The bleeding minotaur. The weeping angel.

Look for all time and you will find only
Cobwebs, shadows, rust – the eschatology
Of dust – the avalanche of History.

It is music, also, moving out across the fluted sea
Or slipping underground – a symphony
Of sound curving back upon itself, then breaking free.

It murders for another tense, another line,
Another key. It is a mantric rhyme
Against the nightmare shredder of indifferent time.

Rises up.
Is what it must be.

Ave Gratia Plena

How love can tear us open and burn
Like quick-lime. Break boundaries. Transgress.
And even after we've declined turn
Back to us, palms open, to shout her *yes*.
She torches conversation, trashes protocol.
LOVE IS, she says, and AVE GRATIA PLENA.
For grace is her province and her will –
And life's not the oppression it was. Never
Again! Things hum now with a soft elation.
He who has hidden himself has lived well –
But not in this case where *annunciation*
Is the only concept and the flying angel
As necessary as the gravity she defies
To proclaim her gospel. Shock of the impossible!

The Dance of Syllables

Love, what is it that makes us listen
So intently? As if after so much history –
Denial, loss, desolation – there could
Be tongues of fire again, crimson scrawls
Of revelation. Not in the march of Progress
But in the dance of syllables... They enter
The ear's portals, the skull's cathedral
To fill the bare aisles, the gutted chapels –
The sad centres of our dereliction. For words
Do not refer to this world easily – yet
They have their music. Surplus. Fierce excess
Feeding the spirit where we live most freely –
In quest. Hovering over fathomless depths.
Out of reach. Torn. Stripped. Flying breathless.

Inner Fugue

When the words come. When the poem strains
Restive at the threshold. When the language riots for its
Freedom. When our first warm milk memories race

Into a time no-one can trace on clock, tv or radio.
When time paces urgently into that other place
Where Eve and Adam disdain to name the rose

And have no cause to name the staring animals
Or emulate their scarlet cries or raucous snarls
Finding their own forsaken calls more musical –

Mortal creatures with angelic cravings!
This is the fugue playing in the double helix
Of our cells, in the archaic alleys of our brain –

Lost and found. Lost and found. And lost again.

Then Love me for my Flying

Remember Leonardo da Vinci? – how as a young boy
He ran through the square unlocking cages
And shouting to the captive birds: *Fly now! Fly now!*
Love, never keep me caged beyond my will

For part of me is like a bird. An albatross –
Born of crag and wilderness – it rises motionless
Above the zig-zag traffic of the tides.
At night it glides across the pack-ice edges

Of the southern hemisphere, wings stretched
Between polluted water and TV satellites.
The zero winds burn clean the toxic air.
This is a shaman's world, a pristine life.

Then love me for my flying – my oceanic eyes –
The whiteness of my neck – my sea-bird cries.

The Song of Words

Water cleans itself until each amber stone
Shines beneath the turbulence: clear, angular,
Eloquent. Even ancient rock and slate and bone

Now yield their natural reticence to chant
The power of water, to sing its lilting essence:
Sa la sa la liea siea – all the way to the distant

Estuary, the jade cormorant, gull's clamour.
We utter more than we can ever know –
For words like water crave the sea, flow under

Our intimate breath, slip under the ticking clock,
Sing in the eyes of the skull, rill in the jaws
Of death – the white spume gashing the rock:

Sa la sa la sa la
Liea siea

CODA

*The Name: there is yet the Name. The Name of the
Beloved cried out in rhythmic throes words the world.*
                                               Gillian Rose

Six Epiphanies

1

Today I hear of a living language
where *poem* and *breath*
are one and the same.

I blow my breath on the window pane
and in the warm moisture
write your name.

The angular letters dissolve
cry down the glass
become invisible again.

2

An end to questions: *what for?* and *why?*
At dawn I hear a severing cry.
It is the voice of Orpheus: *transform or die.*

3

The clock measures other lives not ours.
We sleep through nightmares and wake to new desires –
flames scorching into flames, stars into stars.

4

Loving Aphrodite now keep your distance
that I may find a vacant place
to dance the dance –

that sudden leap through air where outer chance
meets inner grace
and orphan darkness – radiance.

5

Tracing the curve of your neck and small breasts
I am your involuntary witness wanting eloquence
to name your salt-clear eyes, your seagull whiteness –

an intrepid Adam naming the seabirds of the senses,
but when you came in your full nakedness there were no words –
our breathing soared. And sang through the silence.

6

Love listen now and build your shrine in silence.
Did you not know Krishna
adored Radha so as to be alone –

sitting in the blue temple of his solitude
there to blow breath into his bamboo flute –
relishing its emptiness – cadence after cadence

conjuring what did not exist before, phrases
of light, far out and over –
into the encompassing.